UNAPOLOGETIC WORDS

MONICA

ISBN 979-888606595-4

*"This book is dedicated to my beloved child [dog] "**Tzar**". He made me a better as a person."*

*"To my mother **[Prema Bisht]**, who was the most strongest women I came across in my life. I never got a chance to appreciate her but she always believed in me."*

*"To my sister **[Deepa Bisht]**, we were friends and sometime strangers but you are always missed."*

Contents

Contents

Acknowledgements

I want to thank **Vaibhav Singh**. I am so grateful that I found you and now, I cannot even remember the time when you were not in my life. Thank you for supporting my dreams and encouraging me to pursue them and just being there for me.

You been there we me in all phases of my life - the time when I was super chilled out person, fun loving and crazy and then everything turned upside down and I still remember the darkest day of my life, but I find myself laughing and the funniest part is after few days we went on a vacation.

They say, you do not need plenty of friends or bundle of relatives if you have someone who can understand you and have strength to be with you no matter what and that is correct.

You support me like a true friend, you love me like a mother, you protect me as a brother, you spoil me a father and you love me as child. I see every relation in you and still I don't know what you are for me, but I know that I worship you and I believe that if you are there, everything is alright. I am grateful that I have a chance to be with such an amazing person who do not tell me if I am right or wrong but give me an opportunity to analyze and take my own decision.

Thank you for helping me grow as a human and getting the best out of me and being the most supportive partner, I can ever ask for.

Prologue

I had put many thoughts before writing this that how it impacts the feelings of people. Every time, I got the same answer, if the person will survive at the end of the book there will only two results - either you will hate me for disrespecting your long-lived perception or you may find it interesting that at least someone have guts to speak up.

So, I really do not want to hurt anyone, and this is my perceptions on life and everything, what I have seen, what I have felt and what I feel like to share. Again, my perceptions and that could be different from yours and it is totally fine. That is the beauty, we think, we learn, we analyze, and we all know that what is correct and what is not. Someone says, some don't. Some are okay to be a bad guy, and some want to keep a clean image, but all these rights and wrongs are there in our head.

Sometimes, we are afraid to do or speak things because we care about what someone else think. I believe if, everyone has right to share their views and before getting to any kind of conclusion, it is important to understand the views.

We have given a beautiful thing - mind, why not use it sometime and see if we are able to see things differently from someone else's point.

1

Why so Judgemental?

Let's take a situation when we are forced to be with some random person, and we do not like them. We cannot go out, we cannot talk to our known people but just had to spend the entire day, months or year with some random unknown stranger or any annoying person.

Sound like hell...!! I know right.

On day one, may be, we do not like that person, may be on day two, we start to notice that how different that person is - may be a bit messy or noisy or talkative or silent or a cleanliness freak. But after spending few months with them, we might start to explore their side - the side he generally does not show to everyone, the actual side and it was not so bad. Those things which was unbearable at the start might not matter now or may be at some point we even start linking their behavior and unknowingly after some time we might be doing the same stuff as we find it fun.

Nothing has changed with the behavior of another person; it is we who have changed. We loosened ourselves to see the things beyond our comfort zone. We as humans, always judge everything right from the point it comes in front of us, we do not understand, we do not think, and we do not know but we still judge without any proven evidence.

Life is way too big to explore, far bigger than rights and wrongs. The right in your opinion might be wrong for someone else and vice versa. But we close ourselves for any opportunity in which we can explore and which may change our thoughts. We think with our wonderful minds and that is where the things start to go wrong. Whatever we think or whatever our perception is; could be okay for us but that cannot be applied for the whole human race and with that perception we start to judge others so how can we expect a different result.

Every human is unique and different in their own way. Just imagine, what kind of world that would be where every human is just like you, like the exact identical. I bet you cannot survive in that world as well and you are smart enough to know the answer. I heard about a quote sometime back that "when you have a rose garden you grow some thorns as well". But let me tell you, Roses do have thorns, to protect themselves from bugs, animals and humans. These thorns serve the function of keeping any intruders away. So, I guess these thorns are equally beautiful and my point is these different people, with different behavior is the beauty of the world and equally important for the survivall of human race.

My personal perception behind this quote is that every human being is a package of good [s] and bad [s] but we do not know that what is the story behind that "bad" and maybe it's just a "fake bad" used as a shield of protection or maybe not, that person never really got a chance to analyze the "bad". But in order to know the reason, we need to understand the person by leaving ourselves aside and with a motive to learn about them.

Or maybe your goodness can change other person bad [s] to good [s] but for that as well you have to leave your perception aside as the intention should be sharing, gaining and understanding and not to knowingly or unknowing imply your perception on someone.
World/people is so beautiful place when we understand it with open minds, rather than judging and criticizing everything just start to appreciate and understand and if your heart and mind is in right place, you do not need anything else.

2

Are you a Dead Fish?

I have heard many a times that why one must be so serious in life, do mistakes, do whatever you want, live on the edge, do what makes you happy, go with the flow. Correct.

But remember we are not a dead fish. Only a dead fish can go with the flow. Sadly, but true, we are humans and even an alive fish knows where to swim and what to do and therefore, we are far better than that.

It's not bad to enjoy every moment of life, do what makes you happy and be impulsive but every risk we take should be calculative. You cannot just take risk without knowing all the possible outcomes. Let me tell you a beautiful life incident!

One day I was hanging out with my friends and one of them said let's go for a vacation. Others agreed. I said whoa whoa whoa.... I cannot. I am saving up for my car and I cannot go now. They literally argued that - Oh please, that will come, you need to come with us. They booked flights and when I asked that where we gonna live. They answered - we will check after reaching the destination.

Like seriously, we do not know where we will going to stay, since it's a last-minute flight so obviously, it is expensive, what we will do after going there - just hand around like a bunch of hippes and what about using up my savings on something only I want to do just because my friends are doing.

Yes, you are right. No point. It's not unhealthy to plan things in advance. Planning requires a lot of research, and we end up getting ready for any unforeseen things which might or might not happen, but we will be ready. Yeah, I do not support overthinking and just getting worried all the time about everything and think the worst outcome, but at least think

Not only for a trip, but for everything, planning your day, week, trips, finance or life is very essential part of living. It does not mean that you are a boring person. It means you are intelligent enough to get ready for everything. Sometimes, being impulsive if okay but that too is only when you have planned your finance. Yes, finance my dear. Sadly, but true, anything and everything whatever we do need money to have good standards or even live a respectable life otherwise mediocre living is also in these days. More than half of the population is doing that.

As I mentioned above, I heard many people saying that you should not be so serious in life. I may say, don't sit with that grumpy face, no one like that, it's kind of a turn off and no one wants to be around such people who are always angry or grumpy or frustrated but yes be serious in life if you want everyone to take you seriously - in your family, with your friends, in your office or anywhere in public. People don't want to waste their time on anything which is not up to their level, and you may end up being just a time pass for everyone. Being an overthinker or angry does not mean you are serious in your life and neither does being fun loving and saying dumb things mean that you are not serious about life.

You should just know that where you need to be serious and where you do not, let's say, you cannot go to office and be like childish and playful, it is not a correct attitude and being said that you cannot be silent and awkward when you are sitting with a group of friends.

You should be very careful about what you are at what time and at the same time be true to yourself. There is no point to portray a false image of yourself to anyone, do what you mean, and which is healthy as per the situation.

Also, being serious sometimes collided with being wise. No, it does not mean you need to come out wise [in your own head] in front of everyone. Trust me, no one likes to be preached and no one likes a preacher. I would rather suggest being a good listener, have an open mind and thoughts.

So, have you noticed I used the word "suggest" rather than "advice". It was on purpose. No one wants any advice, but if you give them a suggestion, you are giving an opportunity to figure out by themselves.

Just remember, life is all about learn, observe and improve

and it is a never-ending process.

3

Pets are like Family

Yes, they are so cute and adorable that everyone wants them [like cats or dogs] to have someone to cuddle with and they wake you up in the morning with all those wet kisses and follow you everywhere and never leave you alone even for a second but they are not just toys from which we can play and neither it is their duty to make us happy. They are huge responsibility.

It's easy to adopt/get a pet and say that your pet is like your family but it's very difficult to treat them as one. To wake up every morning, even if it is cold winter morning, you need to get up and take them out for a walk, you have to play with them whenever they want, you need to feed them with the best dishes and not just the leftovers, they are not dustbin; they are kids, you need to buy cool clothes for them and get hundreds of toys to play with so that they do not get bored. You must give them so many kisses and pamper them when they are angry. Need to be patient and calm with them and lots of other things. You need to remember that you may have thousands of things to do but they are waiting all time to play with you and that is not much, they deserve it.

Then, why they are treated differently than any other member of your family?

Tell me honestly, can you ever leave your infant child alone in the house or even with any of your relative and go for vacations? Can you ever give your kids leftovers? Will you ask any person in your family to not sit/sleep on sofas or beds only because you need to rearrange it after they get up? Will you go to someone's place if they say that your kids are not allowed? Will you let anyone give lecture or be disrespectful to your kids? Will you leave your kids if they want attention or time or a constant pampering?

No, correct. Then just replace "kids" with your "pets" and then think and you might see the difference.

Having a pet means having an infant for entire life. They never said to bring us, it was your own decision, and that is why you should think before making any decision in your life that are you ready for it because for somethings in life there are no backsies. They are not just a furry toy you play with when you are low. For them you are their entire world, and they deserve each ounce of care, love, respect and attention that any other human deserves.

I was one of them who love puppies and some people around me say that I am not mature person and yes, I never knew what is like to have a pet but when 2 years ago I got my dog named Tzar - German Shepheard, and that day my world changed.

I never understand what the definition of maturity for

everyone is, and how can someone tell if I am mature or not. Like what are the criteria but trust me when I see Tzar, I know what I am. I am Mother, who can go to any limit for her child and trust me, Tzar is the most attention seeking dog I have seen in life. But it's my responsibility to cater his every need. The only place I go for outing is park so that he can play - and that to 3 times a day for more than an hour but I do not have any regret I love to spend my every free second with him. I go to only those places - hotels, cafes, restaurant etc. which is dog friendly, I just want to see him in front of eyes. I changed my job to work from home so that I shall not have to leave him alone and his food is served first than rest of my family. He has his own bed but he still sleeps on my bed and sit right beside me in Sofa when I am doing office work.

I will not say I have done any kind of sacrifice because it is my responsibility. It really feels complete when he is with me.

People use to say that you should occasionally give your dog mutton or otherwise he will not eat any other thing, you should not feed them from your own plate, should leave them alone in the house so that they can be trained to be alone, do not disturb them while eating otherwise they will bite you and blah blah blah.

After being a mother of German Shepheard [which is considered to be an aggressive breed], I think that you cannot generalize the attitude of a dog through their breed. Their attitude completely depends on how you have raised them. Tzar, on other hand have plenty of mutton/buff since childhood that he does not go crazy over food. He eats what he likes and never tries to get angry over food or anything because we have developed such an environment for him and made him feel so superior that he knows that whatever thing is there in the house is for him and he does not have to beg for it. He goes with us everywhere and I he is the most friendly German Shepheard you can ever see.

If I have to tell about Tzar, it will take another full book, so, I am not going to bore you but just want to remind that treat them as the family, as your child and their behavior will reflect your upbringing as in the case of kids.

Disciplining your pet does not mean you have to be harsh on them or treat them as a pet, we don't do such behavior with our kids, right. If you just love them and tell them what is right and what is wrong and give them reason why it is wrong, trust me they understand that better than anyone else and they will show how they respect your decision.

4

Don't mind, I am just Honest!

This is rather the funny one. Your friend got a new haircut or dress and very happily came to you to show it. Your response - what have you done to your hairs, it does not suit you or you look so skinny in that dress. Wow, you made her day, and, in your defense, you say - please don't mind but I am just being honest.

Seriously! No one is interested in your honesty. What good is that honesty if it is hurting someone. Is it really the honesty? Where you have be honest you must have thousands of buried secrets and suddenly you are the preacher of truth. Let me tell you, you, in your own mind think that you are the honest person by criticizing others whereas in reality you are just a negative and jealous person who might get happy in hurting others and these are the person who cannot handle the same honest opinion if someone else give it to them.

There is a huge difference between "being honest" and

"being negative". An honest person always knows when to open their mouth and never intent to hurt anyone whereas a negative person shall throw the garbage on their thoughts in order to make the other person feel small.

My mother used to say a thing I can never forget - "Words are the strongest thing. Those the "words" which will make you the nicest person in the room and those the "words" which will make others hate you forever. It's important to choose your words wisely because it's like the gun you fired, you cannot un-fire it. It is simply not possible. So, when you say something, you just say it you cannot take it back. Whatever comes from your mouth shall be analyzed in your mind and permitted by heart."

It is not okay to say anything you want to say, if you cannot speak good and cannot see the positive things, it is better to keep your negativity to yourself. It is okay to be the dumbest person in the room, but it is not okay to show your wise in the cost of hurting someone's feeling and making them small.

It is actually very hard be nice to everyone, to be happy for everyone and to be always positive but to be a good human it is necessary. The world is full of those kinds of people we do not need them, let's stand different from them and as they say it starts from one person so be that one person.

On the other hand, being kind and positive does not mean you have to shower everything you have; it means you are dumb. People take advantage of your dumbness. Apparently, there is no said rules of being kind but as per my opinion, your kindness is another word for being positive. Try and see the positive side in the most terrible situations and analyze the pros and cons of your doings. Just make yourself stand at the pedestal and assume how do you feel if someone else say those things to you and if you feel okay with it, it should be right and if not then how can you think that it would be okay for anyone else.

It just take few words to hurt someone but sometimes, when we are angry or sad, we tend to say harsh things to the people we love and respect and after sometime we realize but then it's too late, the damage is done. Another person can forgive you but it's the tendency of a human mind that it does not forget anything, maybe it can forget the good but never the bad things. As they say, once the glass is broken, it could be repaired but it shall always have those marks. Feelings are like glass, a person might forgive someone, but the marks shall always remain, and these are the marks only, which change your feeling towards other person.

Trust me, I am also not a person, rather I will say I am the most imperfect person who had also unintentionally or in anger said many harsh things to others and I cannot change it. But it is fine, I cannot just regret on my past forever but what I can do is to make efforts to be more positive and kinder in future. There is always a scope, and it is always a right time to try and be better because as humans we understand the mechanism of inner life and we grow, and it is never too late for anything. It is okay to apologize when it comes from within and when it does you will not repeat the same thing again.

5

Are we really diverse?

India, the land of diversity- culture, traditions, religions etc. 10 people living in a house- 2 are Hindu, 2 are Muslim, 2 are from South Africa, 2 Gays and 2 are from London, we meet each other but Hindu and Muslim are not on talking terms, they do not celebrate Christmas, everyone in the house does not respect Gays and Transgenders, people from London do not like the people from South Africa.

Then does that mean the house has diversity, only because we have different group of people living under one roof. The same scenario is in India, we do say we have diversity, but we are not happy about the other things. We only want to live in the shell we took birth.

When Christmas comes, people say we should not celebrate these things cause our children are not clows and this is not our festival. When Valentine's Day come, they say we should not celebrate this thing rather we should remember this day as a black day of Indian history as we lost many Indian soldiers in Pulwama attack, we should respect Hindi and English as it is a foreign language and there are plenty of other examples like this.

Sometimes, I just think what kind of diverse person these are. People have so much of hatred in their hearts that they just do not want to see the good, the bright side of anything.

It's okay to remember our soldiers but why only remember them on a certain day, certainly whatever happened is wrong, but Saint Valentine has nothing to do with it so why to curse him or that day. Life is full of such bad memories and hard days which are heartbreaking but why not be grateful for the things we do have and appreciate the love. Jesus Christ have not done anything bad for us neither did any black guy or white guy.

If General Dyer killed several people, it's bad but that does not mean that whole Britain is a bad country and seriously many Indians if given a chance will take the first flight to relocate to Britain.

Why do we stare any Gay or Tans and why do we not treat them like any other human. They are also the beautiful creation of Universe and just because they have different sexual preferences or physical appearance than other humans do not mean they are different or aliens and will not be respected.

It is good that one should respect their mother tongue or their own beliefs and preferences, but it is not at all okay to be bad mouth about other things. What are you teaching to the future generations? Nothing that is good for the society or living.

It's too easy to say that we are a diverse nation, but our minds are way too conservative, and we tend to do the same to our future generations by telling them what is good and bad as per our ideology and not giving them an option to analyze things and be different from what we are. The problem is we want to be superior and therefore we are afraid to give our children the options to find themselves because we know that if they will find themselves and have their own thoughts then we can no longer be dominant and no one wants to lose their authority.

The real diversity shall be when everyone - human, animal or any living being are treated equally which mean with the same respect, love and compassion and not just putting everyone in a mixer.

6

Naked Truth

Being a woman, you must have come across with these things at least once in your lifetime, like - these denims are too skin fit, the top is too deep, the dress is too short, the heels are too high etc. When we see a woman, we start judging her with the clothes she wears.

We are okay to see porn and masturbate in the bathroom, we are even okay to watch the Hollywood movies and appreciate their body but when you own wife wear some deep neck top or a short dress, it's not fine. People gets uncomfortable and abusive if they see cleavage of their known female but if someone the cleavage is of some unknown women in public, they tend to stare them so badly and make them super uncomfortable and they are okay to browse naked photographs of females on the net.

What kind of double standard life people live, and they are living it continuously without any rational logic behind it. I really wanted to know sometimes that what kind of sexual satisfaction a cleavage can give. Seriously, it's just a skin of the body. And then comes those people those kind of people that have problem with what a woman wear.

Before, going any further in our discussion, I want to know that who has given anyone any right to

Rather than saying to a woman that what she can wear and what she cannot, why on the earth you not need your males that it does not matter what a person is wearing, you do not have to see and assume unhealthy things.

There was a time that cavemen do not wear anything, does that mean they would have raped every women they see. No, correct. For a sensible human being who have some goals and motives in life, who know that there are many things in this world to explore like countries, animals, universe etc. will not give a single though on what anyone is wearing. Only a focus less person can focus on these things because otherwise what else they can gossip about.

Every woman has a right bc do whatever she wants, go where-ever she like, dress anything she feels okay, eat what she wants without thinking twice about anyone as it's her life, she owns it, and no one has any right to make her feel bad about her choices. She is the most powerful person yet so understanding and one should remember to not exploit her in any way as she is the one who created you and she is strong enough to end you.

7

Finding the Root Cause!

In our everyday life, we see plenty of homeless people on streets begging for money, stray animals with their innocent eyes staring us in the hope of food. These situations really break my heart that how other half of the society is even struggling for a living and then I see those kind humans who feed them. But still it does not make me happy.

I question myself are we really helping them or wanting to get an approval that how kind human we are or just for a self-satisfaction that we have done a good deed and is it really a good deed?

Of course, it's a good deed to feed anyone but no you are not helping anyone. We are just temporarily and that too for an extremely small span of time providing them but giving them a hope that yes, they can survive by this food.

But what about tomorrow or what about the second meal or third meal of the day. Now these people or animals are again on road to beg for living.

Feeding someone is good but not getting to the root cause of the situation is not good and thus you are just self-satisfying yourself that from all the things we have done wrong/bad, we have made up for it. Come on, we are humans, and we are imperfect and in everyday we do lot and lot of things that we shouldn't.

Feeding 10 people/animals one meal a day is not some help. Why don't we get to the root cause? Why people come to another state and beg when they literally can work even a minimal job at their own cities. No one beg at their own city, they come to metros, beg for living, populate and their children beg, and the circle goes on and as a result those people who cannot even afford to survive are populating like anything. Resources are limited but when it must be distributed with the ones who are not an add on to the economy then it's just a liability and some kind humans are giving these liabilities hope that they can survive without hard work. Why do not we educate them about not populating or send them back to their native places and help them find work. Yes, that is hard and permanent solutions but why we will choose that when can get self-satisfactions or redemptions so easily by just feeding them.

And so as the case with stray dogs, they are predators, you are not giving them kgs of mutton thrice a day and the food which give only keep them alive and since they populate in bulk the result remains the same - more strays. Rather than feeding 10 dogs, if you will neutralize only 1 dog, that will be the day you are helping them.

The solution is not to influence people to adopt a dog rather than buying one because it's a choice and everyone is free to have one. You don't adopt a child when want your own right. It's totally an individual decision what they want but how to control the population of these innocent creatures in on our hands.

So better take a right decision, erase the root cause and not fall for temporary solutions just because permanent ones are difficult and tedious.

8

Independent By Choice

Why it is important for men to work their entire life and why it is an option for a women to be a housewife?

Why the men are called providers and why women have right to spend the hard earned money of their husbands/ father on shopping?

Why men need to overlook their passion and do a permanent job whereas women can pursue whatever they want?

Is it really fair for the society wherein we talk about gender equality but we somehow believe that it is the responsibility of men to take care of every needs of a family and to look after everyone financially. When a person go on a date or restaurant, why is the men who pays, it is not the duty of a man pay bill or why a male must plan everything for a vacation and pay for it.

When women these days are equally educated, they have choice to not be a helping hand or pursue their passion and depend on men for the luxurious living. Why women cannot be the providers, why they have an option to destroy their career and depend on a male for living or not even start a career. Now, some will say, they bring a new life and take care of the household. Correct and agreed. But what good is that life you are bringing if one person is only working to financially support that new life. A child needs both parents equally. What is a point of bringing that new life when you are not more than sufficient to raise it without any hassle or without working your ass off? There are kids who do not see their fathers every day, because they go to work when the child is asleep and come after they went to bed at night. What kind of bonding they will have with the fathers. Are fathers only the ATM machine? They too want to talk to children but cannot do because he is also a human and humans do get tired.

It seems like men are born to open a charity service for lazy women and this is the truth of majority of household. Life is not about only work, work and work and women can be the providers, can be a helping hand.

Having children is not a necessity if you are not so well off to take care of that person for at least 20 years without working hard. It is not a responsibility of a mother to raise a child and then we say we do not have that bond with kids. Having kids should be luxury otherwise you are adding just another nobody in the population which sadly is very high enough. Having kids is not an emotional decision, it's the most particle decision of life.

Just imagine that what good that wealth will get if you do not see your partner for days, you do not have moment to sit and talk. Every women expects that they should get attention from their partner, go for outings or evening walks or just spend time together but when men are working their ass off the whole day, it is understandable that he will get tired and might not be much active with the family and on the other hand slowly the family also does not want to spend time with the male provider as they do not have that bond with them.

I am not at all saying that a housewife is not doing anything, because many people have tendency to take the words in a wrong way. Just to clarify, I appreciate a housewife very much, they are the backbone of the family. They make any house a home, but it is not a job of a female to just stay at home and do all the chores of everyday life.

Going out - travelling, talking to people, doing work and much more is tiresome and challenging but in today's fast-growing world in order to maintain a good lifestyle it is important for both to work and earn and take care of household duties as well together.

If both partners are working, half of their life problems shall be solved. They can make their own decision after careful analysis, they will both be financially independent, they shall have their own view point and an understanding/ respect for others opinions, the small day to day problems will be overlooked and hence more peaceful environment.

Being said that, it's the choice which is hard to make as staying at home in a comfortable environment where everything is served in a silver plate and depending for everything on someone else is always easy than going out in market and dealing with strangers with different opinion but they say freedom comes with a price and it's our choice that are we ready to pay the price?

9

We don't talk anymore!

We are socially expressive, we can put thousands of pictures in Instagram, have hundreds of friends in Facebook, willing to talk to any stranger on Tinder but how many of them know the actual you. Or let me re-phrase the question - To how many people you are showing the real version of yourself?

In social media, whatever we do is just for fun, to keep ourself distracted from the actual reality of life and slowly it became our own reality which is indeed a fake reality because I can never believe that there is any person who does not want a peaceful evening, watching sunset, no troubles in mind and talking to someone about the inner you.

The problem is not at all social media, it's the best thing of technology as it connects you with the entire world but the real problem is communication. We have stopped communicating, we have stopped showing your true self, we have forgot that we are humans, and it is okay to be imperfect and yet beautiful.

We think we know a person, but we only know what they are showing us because no one wants to open-up, communicate things and on the other hand no one wants to listen and support. The listener only wants to know thing to get some spicy news or to do their preaching but sometimes we do not want that preaching, sometimes we need someone only to be there and just listen.

People are struggling to find the human connect, just imagine that these days people are paying hundreds of dollars to a psychiatrist and spending hours and hours with them and for what - just to talk, or if not, they are doing suicides or getting into depression or tension which is not sucking the life out of them but also, they find themselves so hopeless and alone. In the world full of people, it's extremely sad that we do not have a single individual from which we can open up and tell them what is going on.

This was not the world, which was created, where people used to have bater system, where people used to make plans and initiate huge revolutions together, where people were important, that was the society I have studied in my books and not the one I am constantly seeing every day.

Who has changed the reality? Who has changed the world? Who made us the person we are today? Why everyone gets depressed so easily?

No one to blame, it's us, it was our choice. We have pushed the people around us so far in the want to be included, in the want to be someone. We are willing to go on a party where we don't know anyone, and no one cares if you are even there but it would be boring for us to spend quality time with our parents and talk to them about how they are managing the household or if they need anything. And then we find ourselves so distant from everyone because it's just a matter of time that the others also give up on you.

We do not know what is going on with someone and when something bad happens we start our own preaching that there should be initiating more counselling, and they should talk to us if they are in a bad shape. But where were these people when someone need them, when one want help, they refuse to give one because they are busy in their own lives. When someone is vulnerable and want help, people do not want to listen their plea but when something bad happen everyone comes with their own preaching - they should have talked to us or we should do counselling. But where were you when you were needed.

Counselling is a regular process, it's a process of talking, it's a process of understanding and analyzing and then working together as a team to overcome it. One should not wait for counselling when something bad happens but what do I know?

When someone take an extreme step - e.g., Suicide, it never happens overnight, it's a process of frustration, disappointment, feeling unworthy and depressed from years and years. Where are these preachers from years and years? They simple do not care. No one care whatever happens to you and that is the sad reality of today's word. Therefore, asking for help is the only solution.

You do not have to be strong always and you do not have

to think twice what others think because those others will never lose a thing without you. You are depressed and you need to get out of that situation no matter what. It is okay be miserable, to be a mess, to be at the lowest point of life and still strong enough to ask for help because there is a good saying in Bhagavat Gita - "God will always help them who help themselves first".

So, take the first step - communicate. Say whatever is there in your heart, shout for help and it is okay to have a pressure and release it. Life will be much peaceful and easy and at the worst what can happen? People will think you are not strong. Why does it matter? At least when your heart is empty you can start evaluating things again and stand up to face every challenges.

10

The Unseen Power

Majority of people call it God; I prefer to say Energy. Neither created nor destroyed, just transfers. Both positive and negative. Sounds like Science huh!

That's my point, Energy is proven God is not, but it does the same thing. When we say "God", it divides us into different beliefs, culture, ideologies and religions but we say "Energy", we are referring to every organism on Earth and beyond. It combines us in a unique way, and it is simple but beyond our imagination.

God is a faith of human that he never sees but believe is strong enough to make everything right, to take away their miseries and someone they can fear so that they can do well in their life. And that is where everything goes wrong. We are so innocent beings that we turn to someone to correct ourselves and in no time, we just devote ourselves in the swamp of belief and faith just to right our wrongs and be healthy and be happy. Then someday, things started getting better in life and the swamp start to suck us in. Who do you think did that? Who is the supreme power beyond everyone who can forgive us? Who?

What do you think? God?

It is YOU. It is always you. You believed in yourself, you worked hard, you do good deeds, you did not hurt anyone intentionally or unintentionally, you were compassionate, you did everything. You corrected yourself. There is no one who is judging or forgiving or rewarding you. It is just, always YOU.

It is possible that the whole world think that you are a good person, and you never did anything wrong to anyone. You portray that image of yours to the world and the world might believe you. But deep in your heart you always know what you are, even if you never tell anyone, you know and that is what eats you or satisfies you. If you have done wrong, your heart knows and it's a fun game of guilt and torcher that it does. You can hide that from everyone and be happy but when you are alone at the night, it will haunt you. And then you pray to God for forgiveness. On the other hand, if you are happy, you never did anything wrong and your heart is guilt free, you may not turn to God. He has no role over them.

As a human, it is quite difficult to act like a human coz at the end we are just so-called human without an ounce of humanity in us. We tend to do everything as per the choices of others - peers, society etc. Let's say, I don't like to drink alcohol but then what I will do in parties. And then I pray to God before going home that please, my parents should not know.

I know the example is quite lame but what is the last thing we have done that we really wanted to do and that did not harm anyone - physically, mentally or emotionally and it selflessly in favour of someone else.

If your deeds are in right place, you will never worship an idol. For you everything is a God, any human, any animal, any tree, any living or non-living thing or just anything. You will be just grateful for everything and from everything and you won't pray, you will just worship.

11

Everyone has a Story!

Whenever we are at the lowest point in our lives, we often think that whatever happen to us is worst that can ever happen to anyone. We will become the victims in our own eyes and want the composer and slowly and steadily, it becomes our habit to play the victim and get our way.

Once you become the victim of your story, you become a parasite. A parasite that sucks all the good things from everyone. People keeps on feeding this parasite due to their kind dumbness, but have you ever given a thought what will happen when the kindness gets over?

Let me give you an example, you have a bucket full of water and you keep on taking water out one glass every day and never bother yourself to fill the bucket, eventually the bucket will empty. Correct. Same things happen when someone is played victim and you keep you showering your love, care, money and everything on them. One day, these things will end because the parasite is not capable of giving anything, they only know how to suck and when you are incapable of giving more, they shall leave you and find some other host.

It is okay to ask for help when you feel low, but it is not okay to make yourself victim of everything. Sometimes things happen which is beyond our control, like people die around us- the one we love but how long you need to be sad about it. Can you be sad and wasted your entire life? Death is inevitable, some die young and some old. But you are the one who is living, you are alive and on the things, we do not have control, how can we mourn about it always.

If the earthquake came it came, you cannot control it, however, global warming might be the issue but that is a separate topic of discussion, if someone die - it's not in your hand. But, if your relationship broke down - it is in your hand, if you did not get a job - it is in your hand, if you did not get good grades - it is in your hand. You do not need to play victim about any of these.

Things which is beyond your control, you cannot be sad about them and for the things which is in your control, you cannot be sad about them either as you are the reason who messed it up. So, in any situation, how can you end up as a victim?

The things for which we become upset are not even the even the real issues of life, but it might be possible that whatever your problem is - it is important for you but everyone have their own stories, their own struggles, ups and downs but beating yourself is not a solution, telling hundreds of people about your issues is not the solution and not telling anyone about what you are going through is also not a solution.

My mother once said that "if you tell your problems - like in relationships or finance or career etc. people will never be sad about it, why will they have not gone through what you are going through and no one can ever understand, some people will not care about it but will be a good listener, however, majority of people are one who just get happiness out of someone else sadness. So why to give such people the spice for life." Selecting the people for communication is also an art of communication otherwise it will be nothing else than a joke for everyone.

It is okay to feel heartbroken at times, to cry your eyes out and scream at the top of your voice but that should not be a never-ending process. We all are humans, and it is okay to feel sad and lonely but for a day or week or a month you can mourn about the things, after that you need to get up wipe your tears, go out of your shell and face the reality and just move on.

When we were small, doing homework was the biggest struggle but then we grew and fell in love, but it does not turn out the way we expect but still we need to find a good job for our own survival and then someday our parents die, and we feel empty, but we have children, and we have some responsibilities. So, these ups and downs are the part of life, and everyone goes through this with their own unique stories but at the end these are just the phases and characters of life and not the life. These characters and your choices shape the story of your life. It comes with all twists, turns and climax but at the end it is your story, you own it.

Life sometimes is not easy and same for everyone but that is the story of life and trust me we do have some hold on the results. It is you who must discover your secret.

12

All men are same!

I heard this one more often than usual, especially when you are in your college days. Every other girl having breakup and cursing the guy saying - all men are same. Sometimes this makes me laugh than being sad for my friend. My mind used to say - how can you compare a single man with the entire population of men on Earth. You cannot genialize things because of your own bad experience at once. There are smart men like Elon Musk, committed and family-oriented men like Mukesh Ambani, romantic men like Shahrukh Khan and successful men like Bill Gates.

So what do you mean by - all men are same, I really do not understand the phrase.

It is fine that you have some bad experience in a relationship and things does not worked out the way you expected and at the to be very specific, all men/women are not the same, it is just that you expected something and it turns out to be different and therefore, it is not the person who should be blamed, it is just that your expectations are not fulfilled.

Yes, expectations but now you will say that when you are in a relationship you expect, you expect from your parents to be nice and give you money and you expect from your girlfriend/boyfriend to give you attention and pamper you, you expect from your dog to come and lick you when you get up in the morning, you expect from your sister to keep your secret etc.

The problem is never with any person, it is with the expectations we have from them and when they are not fulfilled, that person is bad, whatever they do is not up to the mark, because you expected things differently they resulted differently. It is not bad to not expect things, we are humans, and we expect a lot and that is something we can never control. But expecting without seeing the efforts of other person is wrong, it might be possible you are expecting 120 percent from a person, however, the person from which you are expecting has a capacity of 70 percent and by much efforts and struggle the are reaching 95 percent at times. So, a person's capacity is not matched up to the level of your expectation, then it is simple that how can they meet your expectation. They cannot. And that is when we believe that they are not giving efforts, however, they might be giving their maximum effort at that time.

The problem is not with the person, they are giving their best and neither with your expectation, you deserve what you want and capable of giving, the problem is with the person you selected to set your expectation. He does not have enough to fulfill it.

Being said that, these expectations we have, keeps on

changing and renovating - sometimes growing or at decreasing, depending upon the development of understanding in a relation.

Let's say, you meet a person, a complete stranger, at that time, you do not know him and thus you do not expect anything from that so whatever good things they do, just feel like more than enough, just exceeding your expectations and you feel infatuated towards them. Its, not love and in the course of time you start expecting more and more and you start feeling they are not putting many efforts and it started as if the person has changed or they do not love you anymore.

There is no such thing as not loved or love, we have just given the names to our most intense feelings. Let me ask you, how is it possible that you love someone so much that you want to spend your entire life with them when you just met and do not even know the person, however, 10 years down the line, you feel as if they do not love you anymore or the things are not the same as before. The answer is simple, there might be possible that no love ever existed, it was just the most intense feeling of that specific moment that we termed as love because at that time everything was new, and the person has exceeded your expectations but 10 years down the line you came across many ups and downs and responsibilities etc. but the expectations remained the same and hence the differences grow which can lead to separation.

How can we be into many relationships and we love everyone and when it get over we just do not want to be around them, its not just possible. They say love is for eternity and I believe in it because you cannot stop loving your parents even if they scold you and don't give you attention, right? But that love changes when it comes to the partner.

We are humans, again, and we do change, or I will say the better term, evolve. We evolve every moment, what I was like 10 years ago, I am not like that now and will not be 10 years later. We grow, we become what we are today with all the experiences and situations we have faced. So, yes, we do change, we always change for good. But the problem is our expectations do not change, we want to live in the fantasy world and do not want to face the reality and struggle together. We want to find shortcuts; we like to put the blame game, but we just do not want to look inside and question ourselves that is it really worth it?

It is okay to move on if the things do not work out the way you expect but it is not okay to generalize your feelings and close yourself for every opportunity of growth. It is very easy to blame someone else and always be the hero of your story, but it is important to face the reality, realize that I could also be wrong, tell someone that it was your fault, excepting the mistakes.

But if you really want to grow you need to do this, it is not bad to expect but it is really hard to except and then move on.

13

It is not Okay!

I have seen people saying that he just hit me because he was under the influence of alcohol, or she abused because she was angry or he/she cheated because they were not getting attention from the partner or anything. But it is fine, and it must be our fault and we can be a better person and things will change.

No, it's not okay! It's not okay to take things for granted and give reason for the wrong doings. It is not okay to give excuses for your mistakes, it's not okay to be a taker always, it's not okay to blame others for anything, it's not okay to be a coward and it's definitely not okay to accept anything below your morals and ethics.

Sometimes, we overlook another person because we love them. A mother always overlooks the mistakes of the child and go to any lengths trying to protect them from the outer world. Why would I give example of a mother? Because that is the one of the purest relations of your life. A mother will always protect their child from everything, but they will fail as a parent. The job of a mother is not to protect but to be a support of protection. Her job is to make their kids ready to face the world an in the meantime assure them that she will always be there to protect them.

Love is a very strong feeling, if done correctly, it will make you the strongest person of the world and if done wrong, you will be a coward and people will only use you for their advantage.

Only, you love someone so much does not mean it is okay to accept their behavior. It's not love, it's so dumb. Love always make you grow and prosper; it never pulls you down.

Why are you living? Have you every given a thought that what is your purpose on the Earth. What happens is that when you do not try to find the purpose of your own life then the purpose of someone else's life become your life and you start living for them. Now, your life purpose if only to make them happy and satisfied while they try and achieve their purpose. And that is the sole reason that you overlook everything because you do not want to lose the purpose of life, they have given you to make them happy. It's not love, you think it is but trust me it is not.

No one really come in this life with purpose and a purpose cannot mean that you need to have any big achievements in life or go to space or get a national award. We are all were given equal chance to find the purpose, some find, and some don't and those who don't have to depend on someone to give them the purpose and that is why they ready to give up everything for them.

How can you be with someone who hits you when they are

frustrated or drunk? Who has given anyone right to abuse you or cheat you? Why do we not have any self-respect left and why we cannot stand against wrong?

The only answer is purpose, get your own purpose and you will no longer be an employee in someone else's dreams and doings. It is never too late to find yourself and it is always a right time to make the things stop you do not feel right. You cannot be a free, exploited employee for anyone and you do have the courage to make the things your way. There is always a right time, and that time is now!

14

Chance - Give it to Yourself

This chapter is not about my views, it's for you, that what do you think!

Printed by Libri Plureos GmbH in Hamburg, Germany